EASY INTERMEDIATE

Showstoppers BOOK 1

10 ORIGINAL PIANO SOLOS IN PROGRESSIVE ORDER

T0081592

CONTENTS

ISBN 978-1-70511-128-4

Copyright © 2021 by HAL LEONARD LLC
International Copyright Secured   All Rights Reserved

For all works contained herein:
Unauthorized copying, arranging, adapting, recording, internet posting, public performance,
or other distribution of the music in this publication is an infringement of copyright.
Infringers are liable under the law.

Visit Hal Leonard Online at
www.halleonard.com

Contact us:
Hal Leonard
7777 West Bluemound Road
Milwaukee, WI 53213
Email: info@halleonard.com

In Europe, contact:
Hal Leonard Europe Limited
42 Wigmore Street
Marylebone, London, W1U 2RN
Email: info@halleonardeurope.com

In Australia, contact:
Hal Leonard Australia Pty. Ltd.
4 Lentara Court
Cheltenham, Victoria, 3192 Australia
Email: info@halleonard.com.au

Preface

From my first piano lessons as a child, I fell in love with music. Exploring this beautiful and creative world of music has kept me challenged throughout my life. Music is the best gift that we can give ourselves and our children. Whether this book is for you, a friend, or a student, I hope you continue your musical journey throughout your life and pass it on to others by playing and listening. The piano can be the forever friend you need in times of joy and stress. I hope you enjoy this book and will always keep piano a part of your life!

– Jennifer Linn

Jennifer Linn is a multi-talented pianist, composer, arranger and clinician. As a clinician, she has presented workshops, master classes, and showcases throughout the United States, Canada, and India. From 2009-2019 she held the title of Manager–Educational Piano for Hal Leonard LLC, the world's largest print music publisher. Ms. Linn is the editor and recording artist for the award-winning *Journey Through the Classics* series and the G. Schirmer Performance Editions of *Clementi: Sonatinas, Op. 36, Kuhlau: Selected Sonatinas*, and *Schumann: Selections from Album for the Young, Op. 68*. Her original compositions for piano students frequently have been selected for the National Federation of Music Clubs festival and other required repertoire lists worldwide.

Ms. Linn's teaching career spans more than 30 years and includes independent studio teaching of all ages, as well as group instruction and piano pedagogy at the university level. She received her B.M. with distinction and M.M. in piano performance from the University of Missouri–Kansas City (UMKC) Conservatory of Music where she was the winner of the Concerto-Aria competition. She was named the Outstanding Student in the Graduate piano division and given the prestigious Vice Chancellor's award for academic excellence and service. In 2013, the University of Missouri–Kansas City Conservatory of Music and Dance named Ms. Linn the UMKC Alumnus of the year. In 2020, she was presented with the Albert Nelson Marquis Lifetime Achievement Award as a leader in the fields of music and education.

About the Jennifer Linn Series

Each book in the *Jennifer Linn Series* will feature a wide variety of either original piano compositions or popular arrangements. The music is written in a **progressive order of difficulty**, so pianists of any age can enjoy their music with the added benefit of a gradual challenge as they advance to each new piece in the book. The *Jennifer Linn Series* includes five levels:

Early Bird books feature pre-staff notation with note names printed inside the note heads. The font size is large, and the book is in a horizontal format. Optional teacher or parent duets (in small font) are included. This level is for the beginner who has not yet learned to read notes on the staff.

Easy Elementary features the simplest, single-note Grand Staff notation in a large font size. This level is for the beginning pianist just learning to read notes on the staff and is printed in a regular vertical format.

Elementary+ books include melody with harmony for both hands and includes more rhythm choices and a larger range of keys. This book is for the progressing student who has two to three years of experience.

Easy Intermediate is similar to Hal Leonard's *Easy Piano* level but includes pianistic accompaniment patterns and more advanced rhythm notation as required.

Intermediate+ is for advancing pianists who have progressed to the Piano Solo level and enjoy lush accompaniments and stylistic original compositions and arrangements.

Rainbow Dreams

Jennifer Linn

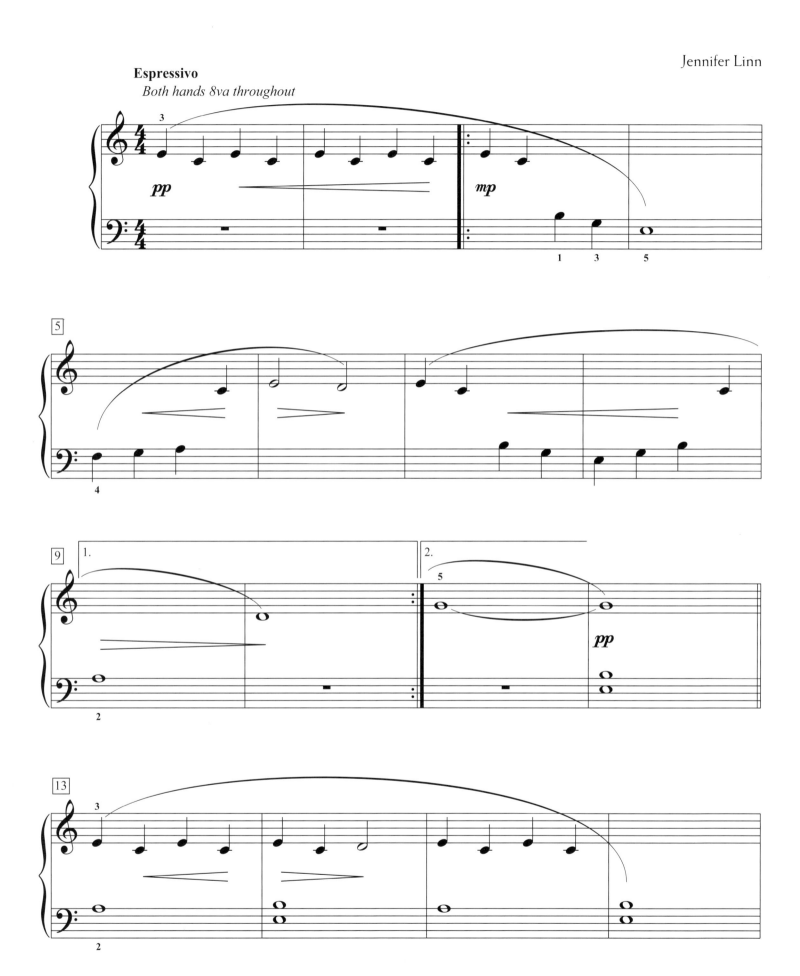

Copyright © 2020 by HAL LEONARD LLC
International Copyright Secured   All Rights Reserved

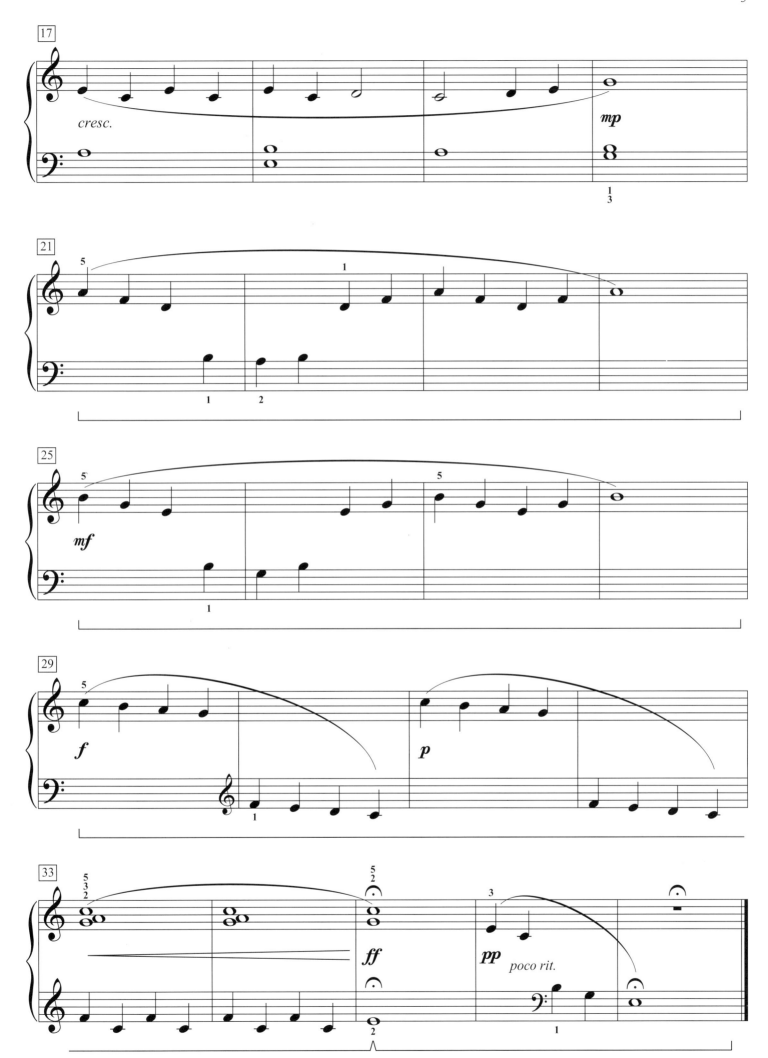

Bluebird Lullaby

Jennifer Linn

Dolce cantabile

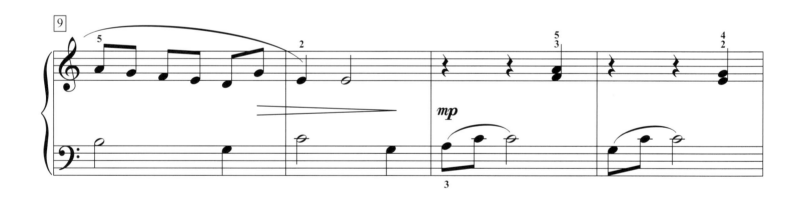

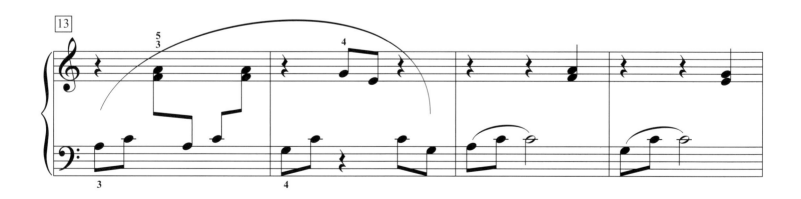

Copyright © 2020 by HAL LEONARD LLC
International Copyright Secured   All Rights Reserved

Tricky Traffic

Jennifer Linn

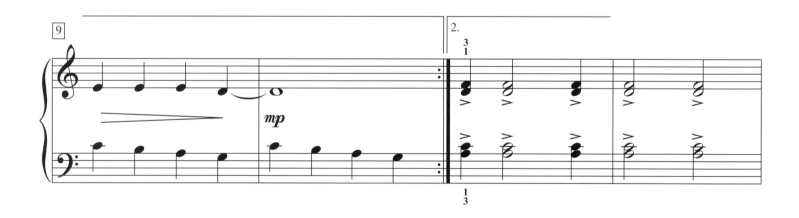

Copyright © 2020 by HAL LEONARD LLC
International Copyright Secured   All Rights Reserved

A Sprinkle of Rain

Jennifer Linn

Copyright © 2020 by HAL LEONARD LLC
International Copyright Secured   All Rights Reserved

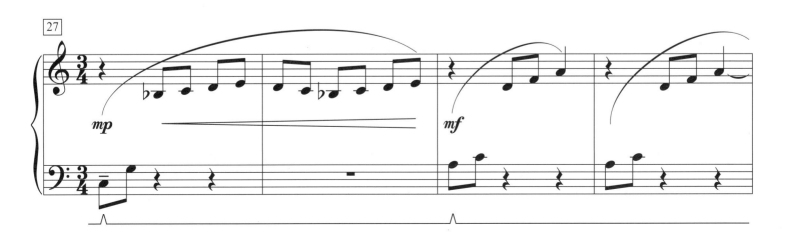

12

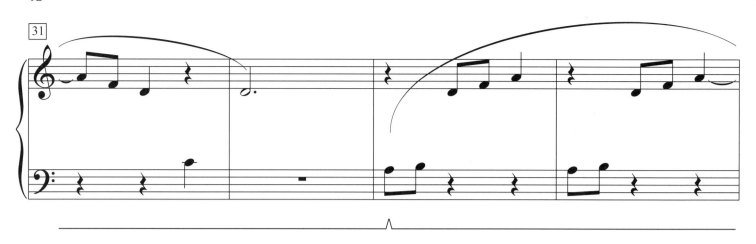

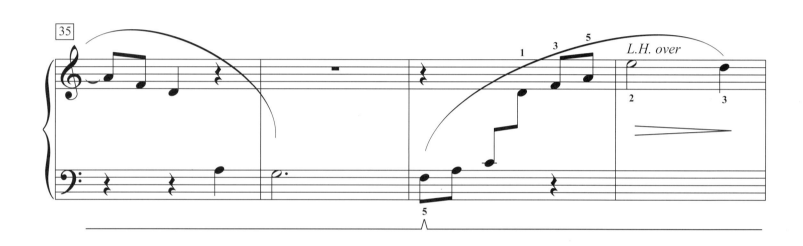

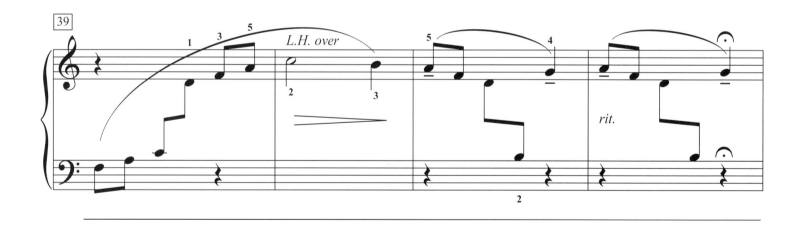

Tiger Chase

Jennifer Linn

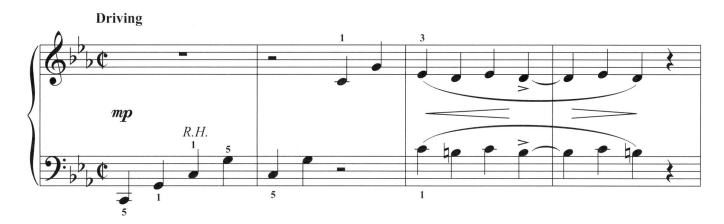

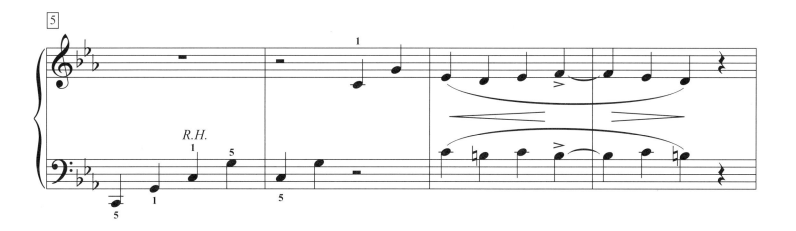

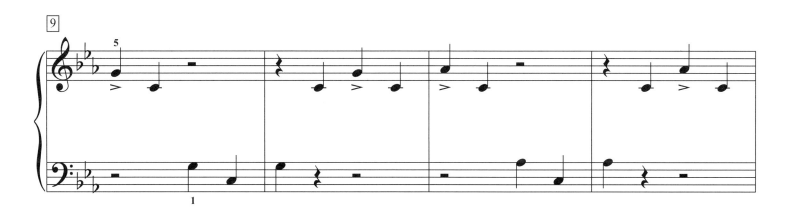

Copyright © 2020 by HAL LEONARD LLC
International Copyright Secured   All Rights Reserved

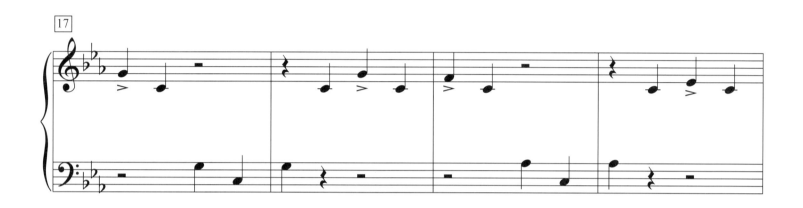

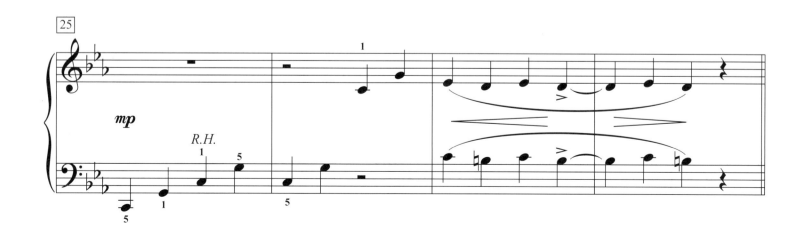

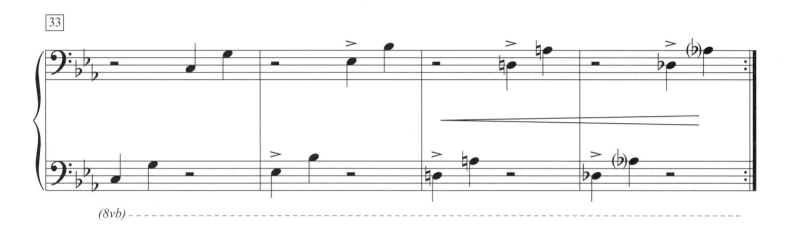

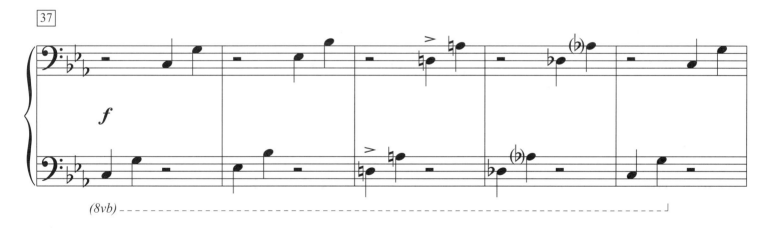

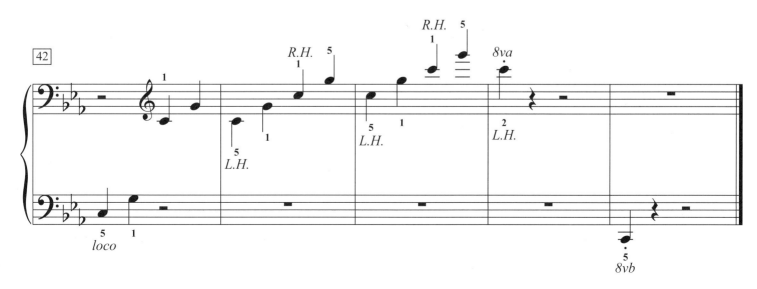

Stargazer Suite
1. Black Hole

Jennifer Linn

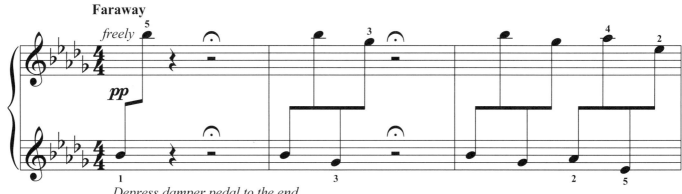

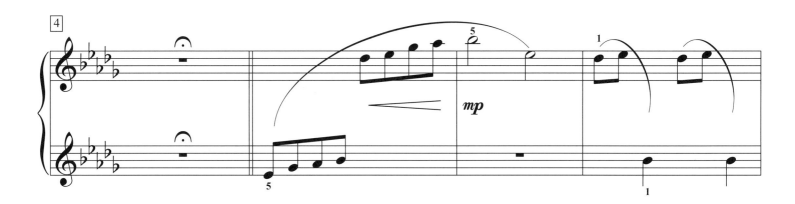

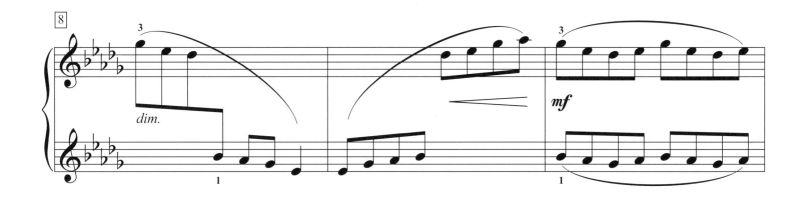

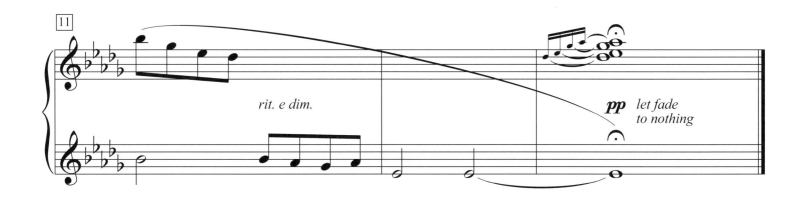

Depress damper pedal to the end.

Copyright © 2020 by HAL LEONARD LLC
International Copyright Secured   All Rights Reserved

Stargazer Suite
2. Falling Star

Jennifer Linn

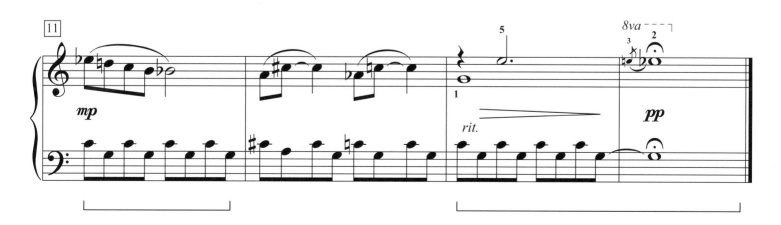

Copyright © 2020 by HAL LEONARD LLC
International Copyright Secured   All Rights Reserved

Stargazer Suite
3. Lost Star

Jennifer Linn

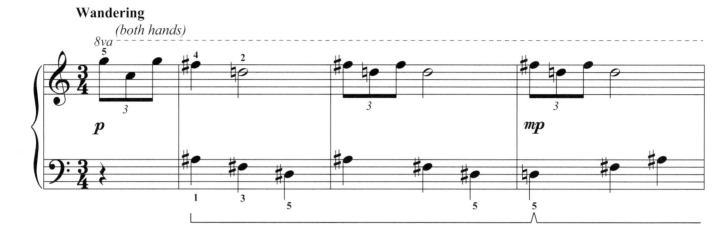

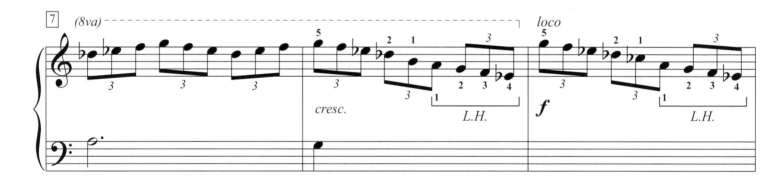

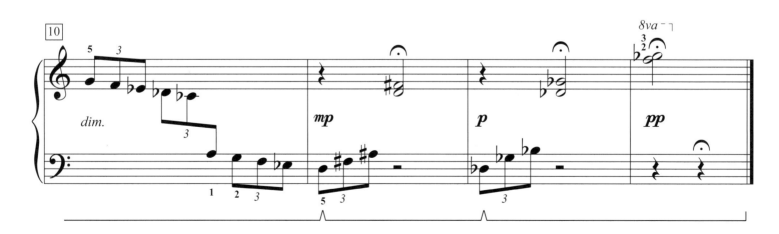

Copyright © 2020 by HAL LEONARD LLC
International Copyright Secured   All Rights Reserved

Stargazer Suite

4. Supernova

Jennifer Linn

Con fuoco

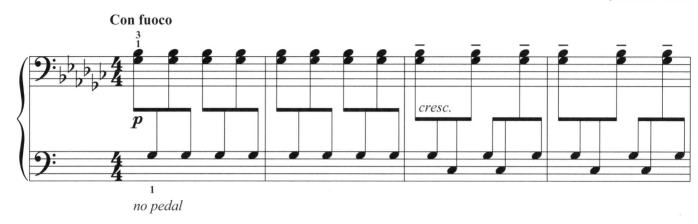

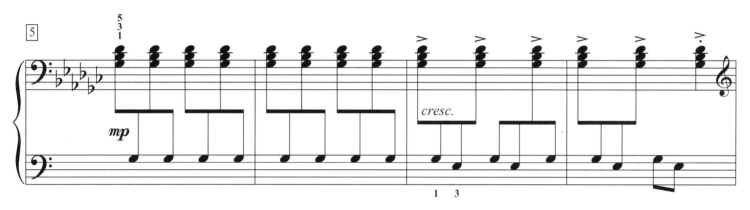

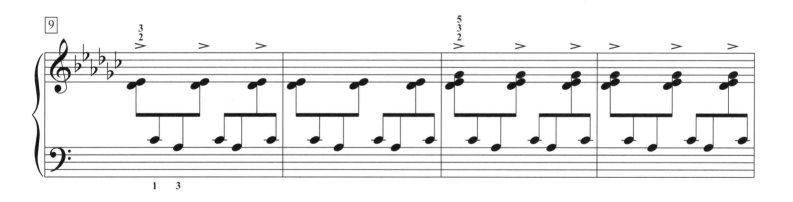

Copyright © 2020 by HAL LEONARD LLC
International Copyright Secured   All Rights Reserved

Prelude to the Brave

Jennifer Linn

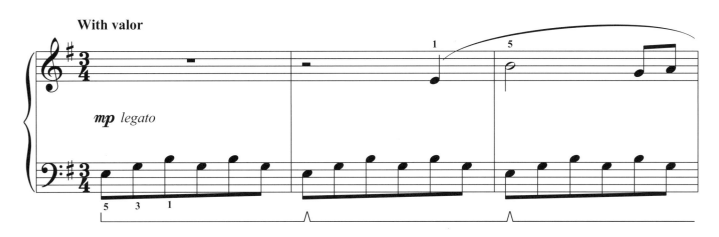

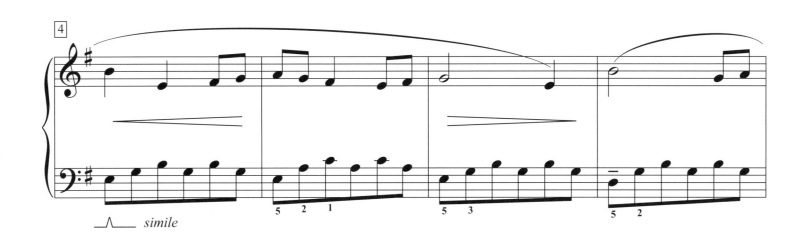

Copyright © 2020 by HAL LEONARD LLC
International Copyright Secured   All Rights Reserved

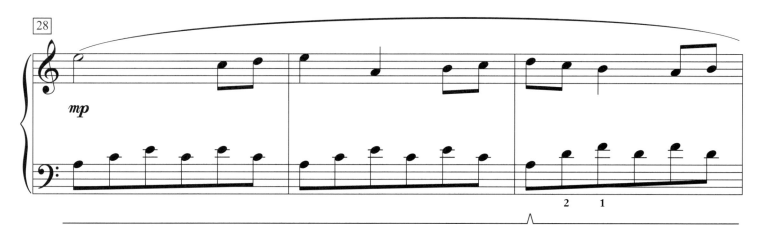

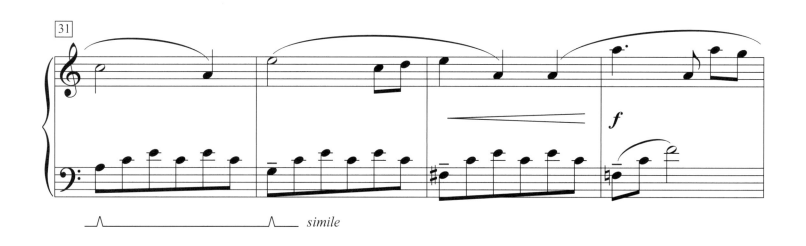

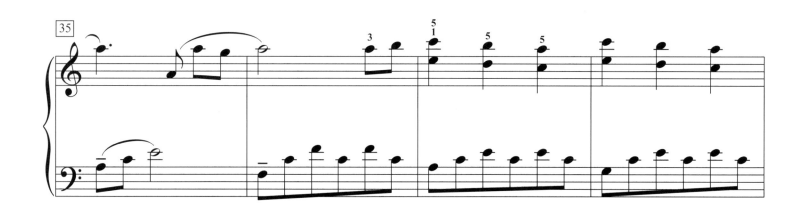